STEM CAREERS

CIVIL ENGINEER

by Nikole Brooks Bethea

pogo

Ideas for Parents and Teachers

Pogo Books let children practice reading informational text while introducing them to nonfiction features such as headings, labels, sidebars, maps, and diagrams, as well as a table of contents, glossary, and index.

Carefully leveled text with a strong photo match offers early fluent readers the support they need to succeed.

Before Reading

- "Walk" through the book and point out the various nonfiction features. Ask the student what purpose each feature serves.
- Look at the glossary together. Read and discuss the words.

Read the Book

- Have the child read the book independently.
- Invite him or her to list questions that arise from reading.

After Reading

- Discuss the child's questions. Talk about how he or she might find answers to those questions.
- Prompt the child to think more. Ask: Do you know anyone who works as a civil engineer? What projects has he or she been involved in? Do you have any interest in this kind of work?

Pogo Books are published by Jump!
5357 Penn Avenue South
Minneapolis, MN 55419
www.jumplibrary.com

Library of Congress Cataloging-in-Publication Data

Names: Bethea, Nikole Brooks, author.
Title: Civil engineer / by Nikole B. Bethea.
Description: Minneapolis, MN: Jump!, Inc., [2017]
Series: STEM careers | Audience: Ages 7-10.
Includes bibliographical references and index.
Identifiers: LCCN 2017002412 (print)
LCCN 2017002884 (ebook)
ISBN 9781620317150 (hardcover: alk. paper)
ISBN 9781624965920 (ebook)
Subjects: LCSH: Civil engineers–Juvenile literature.
Civil engineering–Vocational guidance–Juvenile literature.
Classification: LCC TA149 .B485 2017 (print)
LCC TA149 (ebook) | DDC 624.023–dc23
LC record available at https://lccn.loc.gov/2017002412

Editor: Jenny Fretland VanVoorst
Book Designer: Michelle Sonnek
Photo Researcher: Michelle Sonnek

Photo Credits: Alamy: Monty Rakusen, 9. Getty: Noel Hendrickson, 14-15. iStock: pixhook, 17. Shutterstock: demarcomedia, cover; Aila Images, 1; EmBaSy, 3; Ververidis Vasilis, 4; Tooykrub, 5; Jorg Hackemann, 6-7tl; Darryl Brooks, 6-7tr; Andrey Armyagov, 6-7bl; Anton Foltin, 6-7br; Tom Wang, 8; Brian Goodman, 10-11; sirikorn thamniyom, 16; pjcross, 20-21; Astarina, 23; iko, 23. SuperStock: Image Source, 12-13; Blend Images, 18-19.

Printed in the United States of America at Corporate Graphics in North Mankato, Minnesota.

TABLE OF CONTENTS

CHAPTER 1

WORLD BUILDERS

Civil **engineers** help shape our world. They **design** the roads you drive on. They design the bridges you cross.

Have you been to an airport or railroad station? If so, you've seen their work.

Civil engineers design the structures that support our society and keep us safe.

They make **foundations** strong. They make sure skyscrapers stand against **forces**.

They design the plants and pipes that keep our water clean.

They design tunnels and dams, too.

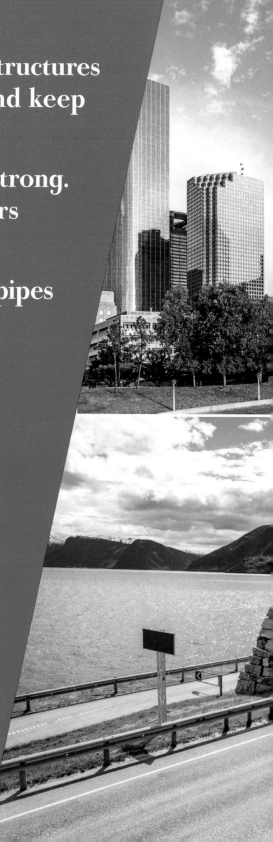

skyscrapers

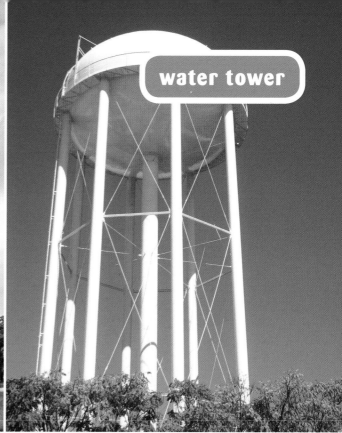

water tower

tunnel

dam

CHAPTER 2

WHAT DO THEY DO?

Civil engineers make **field** visits. They review the site before design begins. They collect data. They **survey** the property.

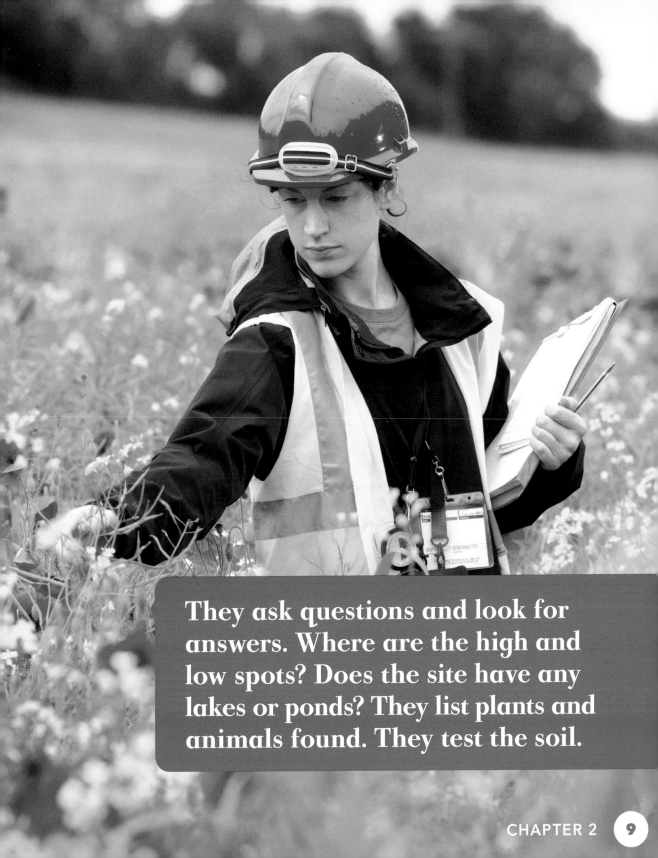

They ask questions and look for answers. Where are the high and low spots? Does the site have any lakes or ponds? They list plants and animals found. They test the soil.

Civil engineers also work in offices. They figure weights, forces, and flows. They figure speeds and energy. They use computers to **draft** plans. They write **specs**. Builders follow the specs to make the project.

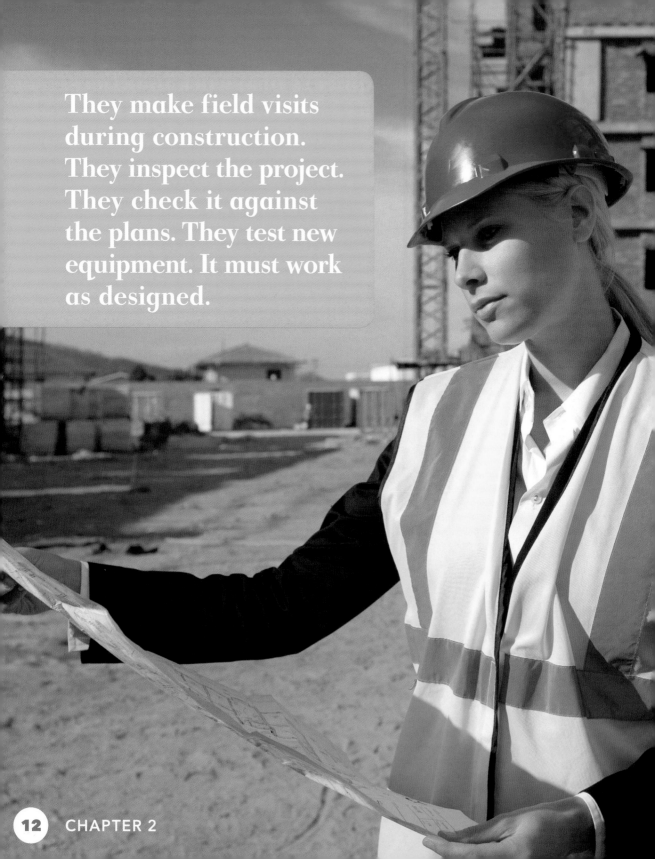

They make field visits during construction. They inspect the project. They check it against the plans. They test new equipment. It must work as designed.

TAKE A LOOK!

How do engineers solve problems? They use the engineering design process.

1 State the Problem

2 Generate Ideas

3 Select a Solution

4 Build the Item

5 Review

6 Present Results

Civil engineers work with people in many other careers. They work with **architects** on building plans. **Surveyors** help with site plans. **Geologists** do soil tests. **Chemists** test the water.

They work with other engineers, too. **Mechanical** and **electrical engineers** help design equipment.

CHAPTER 3

BECOMING A CIVIL ENGINEER

Do you want to be a civil engineer? You must be a problem solver. And you must have strong math and science skills.

First you'll need a college degree in engineering. Then you must get work experience. You must pass a test to become **licensed**.

For now, keep your grades up. Join a robotics team. Do a science project. In high school, you will need chemistry and physics. You will need as much math as you can take.

DID YOU KNOW?

To work as a civil engineer, you need STEM skills. What does STEM stand for? Science. Technology. Engineering. Math. STEM careers are in demand. They pay well, too.

Civil engineers will shape our future. How?

Our population is increasing. We need more clean water.

Cities are growing. We need more electricity.

Bridges and buildings are aging. They need improving.

Do you like math and science? You could help find solutions. You could be a civil engineer!

ACTIVITIES & TOOLS

EARTHQUAKE ACTIVITY

Civil engineers design structures to be strong. In some regions, buildings must survive earthquakes. In this activity, you will build a structure to withstand damage from a pretend earthquake.

You Will Need:

- 30 toothpicks
- 30 miniature marshmallows
- pan of prepared Jell-O

❶ Using the toothpicks and marshmallows, build a structure at least two toothpicks tall. You may construct your structure using squares or triangles or both.

❷ Place your structure on the pan of Jell-O.

❸ Tap the sides of the pan. Does your structure stand?

❹ Next, gently move the pan back and forth. Is your structure still standing?

❺ If your structure needs improvements, redesign and retest!

GLOSSARY

aqueducts: Channels that carry water.

architects: People who design buildings and advise in their construction.

chemists: Scientists who deal with the composition, structure, and properties of substances and with the changes that they go through.

design: To think up and draw the plans for something.

draft: Draw.

electrical engineers: People who use math and science to deal with the practical applications of electricity.

engineers: People who use math and science to solve society's problems and create things that humans use.

field: An area outside a laboratory, office, or factory where work is being performed.

forces: A push or a pull.

foundations: The bases upon which buildings or structures are built.

geologists: Scientists who study the history of Earth and its life as recorded in rocks.

licensed: Officially authorized to practice in a particular discipline.

mechanical engineers: People who use math and science to deal with tools, machinery, and the application of mechanics in industry.

specs: Short for "specifications," these are detailed descriptions of the design and materials used to build something.

survey: Use special tools to gather information, including the exact size, shape, position, and features of an area of land.

surveyors: People whose job is to gather information on an area of land.

INDEX

TO LEARN MORE

Learning more is as easy as 1, 2, 3.

1) Go to www.factsurfer.com
2) Enter "civilengineer" into the search box.
3) Click the "Surf" button to see a list of websites.

With factsurfer, finding more information is just a click away.